GOD'S PROMISES FOR HEALING

30 DAYS OF HEALING SCRIPTURE & FAITH AFFIRMATIONS

―――

Dorita C. McDaniel, M.S. Ed

"My Words are medicine to all their flesh."

Proverbs 4:20-22

God's Promises for Healing: 30 days of Healing Scripture & Faith Affirmations

Copyright © 2021 by MLC Legacy Publishing
Northfield, Ohio 44067-2053

Publisher: MLC Legacy Publishing
Editorial Director: Genriel Santiago
Designer: Genriel Santiago

God's Promises for Healing
Copyright © 2021 by MLC Legacy Publishing

All rights reserved. No part of this book may be reproduced or transmitted in any form or by any means without written permission from the author.

Printed in USA

Contents

Dedication	6
Acknowledgements	7
A Message From the Author	8
Introduction	10
It Is Well!	12
I Am Healed	17
It Is Written	20
Speak Life	25
Prayer for Healing & Deliverance	28
30 Days of Healing Scriptures	30
The Lord's Prayer	61
Psalm 23	65
Salvation Prayer	68
Healing Prayer	70
Index	72
Notes	75
About the Author	81

This book is dedicated to the memory of
ALL the ancestors that came before me.
I AM FOREVER thankful for your light and guidance…
I feel your constant presence.
Granddaddy Meachino & Granny Lois, the Best Grandparents
Mama Doris, Daddy Floyd & Auntie Rolena
Every single day.
I feel your love, guidance, and the wisdom
of your instructions.
Simply Thank you!

To my husband and best friend, David, you have always believed in my dreams. I am forever grateful for all of your words of encouragement when things got rough. Your prayers have carried me throughout this journey and it is appreciated.

Lauren, Dajzsa, Pierre, Deloreon, my inspiration and a mother's joy! This would not be complete without any of you. Hey Lauren, I am so glad you pushed me to the very end…It took me a little while…lol! I can still hear you say, "Mama, finish the book"!

Rita ♡

A message from the author

This book is carefully written to give you the strength to endure whatever battle you are facing. Stay in prayer, keep the faith and never give up! God wants you healed, so claim your healing and begin to praise God, and rejoice that you are restored, delivered, and set free from the hands of the enemy! The Lord wants you to seek Him for your every need. Trust God and believe with confidence that your requests have been heard, and He will answer because our God is faithful!

Prayer is our intimate conversation with Jesus, it allows Him to intercede on our behalf and turn the troubled situations around. Never underestimate the power of prayer! Remember, every spoken word has the power to heal and restore. Keep praying, believing, and expect a breakthrough that the Lord richly blesses you abundantly with divine health!

Let's pray:
Father, your Word says, If I abide in you, you would abide in me; I am standing on your promises, according to, 1 Corinthians 15:57; thanks be to God, who gives us the victory, and in faith, I pray and agree with the expectation that by His stripes I am healed, (Isaiah 53:4-5). I stand in prayer for believing and claiming God's promise according

to Matthew 18:18-20 "Whatever you shall bind on earth shall be bound in heaven; and whatever you loose on earth shall be loosed in heaven. Again, I say to you, that if two of you agree on earth about anything that they may ask, it shall be done for them by My Father who is in heaven, where two or three have gathered together in My name, there I am in their midst."

In the name of Jesus, I ask and pray, Amen.

Introduction

God's Word is medicine to our flesh. Your healing is delivered through a consistent prayer life built on trust and faith (Habakkuk 2:4) and meditating on the Word of God, day and night (Psalm 1:2). I want to convey how important it is to speak the precise scripture to activate God's anointing and healing power. In God's Promises for Healing, I'll share the manifestation of my personal experience, and encourage you to trust God's promises in His Word for deliverance and healing.

Whose report will you believe?
In my years of working in the medical profession, I've met countless individuals suffering from medical conditions and situations that even their doctors said they're beyond repair. It troubled me to watch them resign to the doctor's final report! I would always feel the need to share a scripture from the great physician and send a silent prayer that God would intervene.

The words you say, hear and believe will affect your health; that's why it is critical to start a daily regimen of reading the scripture and studying God's Promises—The Holy Bible. Blessed are those who hear the word of God and obey it (Luke 11:28), and begin to practice speaking wellness and faith affirmations over your life.

Take time to seek God and enter into His presence for Jesus says, "if you ask the Father for anything in [His] name, [God] will give it to you" (John 16:23). The Bible tells us, "when you pray, go into your room, and when you have shut your door, pray to your Father who is in the secret place; and your Father who sees in secret will reward you openly" (Mathew 6:6). He calls you healed and blessed (James 3:10) and promises to give you back your health and heal your wounds (Jeremiah 30:17).

I pray that God's promises for Healing will spiritually encourage and uplift you, the reader, and increase faith that God hears and answers prayer, and the Almighty Father knows our needs before we ask.

Claim your healing and be blessed!

One

It Is Well!

*"Daughter," he said to her, "your faith
has made you well. Go in peace."
Luke 8:48 NLT*

"If I can just touch his robe, I will be healed," the sickly woman said, trying her best to reach and be able to touch the Man's robe. As she pressed against the crowd, she makes her way towards this Man who can heal her. The fragile woman had suffered from bleeding for twelve years, spending all her money on many physicians, but none could make her well. She grew worse and felt much agony as the days went by. Now that the said Man traveling was rumored to cure the sick, it has been the only thing that pushes her to live her days until this Man appears before her and touches his robe.

This story reminds me of my own personal healing testimony.

I had experienced illness before but nothing quite like this! What an initial doctor diagnosed as a typical pregnancy miscarriage requiring just a few days of bed rest turned out to be a much more serious and life-threatening condition. The doctor and his staff continued to reassure me the symptoms I felt would subside and

I would be okay, I was just experiencing the shock of losing a child.

When I finally got home and laid down to rest, I struggled to get comfortable. I felt as if my life was slipping away. The strange sense of doom was gradually creeping over me. My intuition felt a sense of urgency to seek further medical attention, I immediately chose to listen to my body because something was terribly wrong. I called my regular Obstetrics and Gynecologist explaining the backstory and my concerns when she suggested I go directly to the emergency room "ER" with her requisition to be re-evaluated for a second opinion.

Upon arriving to the ER, I was greeted by a young and enthusiastic doctor that specialized in high-risk feminine conditions presented a visibly troubled look of concern and urgency to help me. Per our conversation and chief complaints, he began to run several tests and two different types of ultrasounds that had not been done with the original doctors.

As I wait with my husband and 3 young children in the waiting room, I prayed and tears flowed down my face; I knew something was wrong. The doctor came into the room with an anxious look on his face. He told me I was still pregnant and I said, "Okay, but why am I bleeding?" He said, "The baby is attached to your cervix." According to him, this is a rare case. I have only read of two cases, one died and the other lived, but required a total hysterectomy to stop the hemorrhaging. I will never forget the doctor's face and the words he said to me, "You have a 50/50 chance of pulling through this surgery. The cervix is an area that can cause blood loss we may not be able to control."

I felt tears flowing, I was devastated! Scared beyond words, my children had no idea just how close to death I was. Immediately, I was sent to the surgical unit for surgery. I always keep my bible in my purse, but now, I kept it in my hands and just prayed every healing prayer I could remember. "I called on the name of Jesus!"
I overheard a nurse laughing and talking to the staff saying, "Do you hear her talking to herself?" They were laughing, but I paid no heed and kept praying and asking God to be my surgeon and heal my body in the mighty name of Jesus!

Relating it to the story of the woman with the blood issue in Luke 8:43-48 who had great adversity and affliction for her to have her healing, I was greatly reminded of what my situation was. In which she was in a hopeless situation as well. In their culture, blood issues or any bodily fluid diseases make them ceremonially unclean. Meaning, they can never enter or get close to the temple, at the same time, nobody should touch them or even be close to them. Her hemorrhaging issue cuts her off from any social and religious gatherings. She became an outcast and was forced to be isolated. Her illness makes the situation worse, wherein they would've stone her to death if they knew she was ceremonially unclean. That's why she's silently and carefully walking her way to Jesus, the Man who wears the robe she badly wants to touch, but Jesus already knew that. I think, Jesus was expecting and patiently waiting for her.

Coming up behind Jesus, she touched the fringe of his robe. Immediately, the bleeding stopped. "Who touched me?" Jesus asked. Everyone denied it, and Peter said, "Master, this whole crowd is pressing up against you." But Jesus said, "Someone deliberately touched me, for I felt healing power go out from me." When the woman realized that she could not stay hidden, she began to tremble and fell to her knees in front of him. The whole crowd heard her explain why she had touched him and that she had been immediately healed. "Daughter," he said to her, "your faith has made you well. Go in peace." (Luke 8:44-48)

God wants you well, too. He who made the bleeding woman, as well as, In the beginning, He is the Word and the Word was with God and the Word was God, His Name is Jesus and He invites us to pray; the bible tells us to pray without ceasing. God wants everyone to be in good health. The scriptural prescription for living a long, healthy, and happy life is found in Proverbs 17:22; "A cheerful heart is a good medicine, but a broken spirit saps a person's strength." Jesus spoke the words, "I will remove sickness from your midst, I will fulfill the number of your days", (Exodus 23:25-26). Nothing will happen until you speak in faith and declare with your tongue, "I am healed!" You must walk in deliverance and take authority over the sickness, and command that pain and illness to leave your body.

God promises the length of our days is 120 years (Genesis 6:3), and His Word will never change, the Lord is the same yesterday, today, and forever (Hebrews 13:8). He is faithful to His Word and cannot lie. God is in the healing business, so start believing and standing in agreement that He is releasing His healing spirit in your situation, and all that's left for you to do is to declare that *it is well.*

Two

I Am Healed

For He healed many, so that as many as had afflictions pressed about Him to touch Him. And the unclean spirits, whenever they saw Him, fell down before Him and cried out, saying, "You are the Son of God."
Mark 3:10-11 NKJV

After 2 hours of surgery. I opened my eyes, and the doctor was smiling, saying, "It was a success! I am amazed at how well you did. The bleeding just stopped on its own. We will keep you under observation for 2 days and you'll be ready to go home!"

I am healed!

According to the letter of James in chapter 2, verses 14 through 26, faith without works is dead. Healing requires the foundation of believing that God will deliver you out of that sickness.

In a conversation with my surgeon, he said I would have died if I had not come in for a second opinion. If I had gone to sleep and not returned to the emergency room I would have bled to death and never woke up. I knew that something was wrong, and there's an urgency to have a second opinion. Though it was even worse, I trusted God and prayed upon hearing the bad news. It says in Psalm 112:1, 7, "Blessed are those who fear the Lord, who find great delight in his commands... They will have no fear of bad news; their hearts are steadfast, trusting in the Lord."

In the act of prayer, our wholehearted trust and faith in God is the key component to release healing power. Like a water faucet, faith won't flow unless you turn on the nozzle. In the book of Luke 8:25, Jesus asks the question, "Where is your faith?" If he brings it up that means it's very important! For without faith it clearly says it is impossible to please Him. I know that faith was never the easiest way, nor a lifestyle anyone can live by, but it is the best way to live. As we experience God every day, we get to learn how to trust, honor and please Him. Remember that faith pleases God!

During my follow-up with my surgeon, he was still amazed at the outcome of this critical surgery. He told me this issue was rare and I shouldn't be afraid to have more children. Surprisingly a year later, I was able to give birth to our youngest daughter. Although I had serious surgery, the blood loss and the disorientation I felt was like my life was slipping away. I can't explain it. It was a very surreal and uneasy feeling. But no pain.

Building our faith is a non-stop process that requires obedience, diligence, and complete trust in God with daily meditation on His principles; the Holy Bible reveals that healing requires faith. It is important to keep in mind that faith doesn't just take away all sickness, but ultimately enriches your relationship with God, especially during your pain or sickness. With that, you must feed your faith a steady diet of Scriptures; the Bible says, "Faith comes from hearing and hearing by the Word" (Romans 10:17). While in Galatians 3:13, "The righteous man shall live by faith". To be able to activate, live your faith, and take Him at His word; believe, and trust your request has already been answered.

Regardless of what your eyes can see or the body feels, you must walk, take your divine health, and declare that you are healed in Jesus' Name.

Three

IT IS WRITTEN

He said, "If you listen carefully to the Lord your God and do what is right in his eyes, if you pay attention to his commands and keep all his decrees, I will not bring on you any of the diseases I brought on the Egyptians, for I am the Lord, who heals you."
Exodus 15:26 NIV

The word of God is a treasure chest of promises addressing every life-altering situation. Such evidence can be found when God self-revealed one of His attributes to the Israelites in Exodus 15; it is also one of the many names of God, Jehovah-Rapha. This chapter of Exodus contains a lot of rich details about God and the people of Israel. However, before this chapter, the Israelites were running from a rushing pursuer. Imagine this with me for a while: There's a wind blowing fiercely to every location, they were running crazy, and some were leaving their belongings just to flee from the Egyptian army. You can imagine that there were shouts of desperation, a battle cry, and the horses' feet echoing. Both the people of Israel and the army were running and hasting through the enormous walls of water, and as the Israelites reached the solid ground, the walls of water started to collapse back into the seabed. From left to right, the Egyptian army hurriedly flees for their lives as the wall of water rushed down to bury them. As the people of Israel watched the Egyptian army run towards the solid ground, they sang.

This is a historical event for the Israelites, the moment where God delivered them from the hands of Pharaoh and his army. Exodus tells us the story of Israel being set free from slavery. It is important to understand this story because it is also our story, a story of redemption and restoration. Moreover, it is in this very chapter of Exodus where God promised healing and wellness to the Israelites, and also for us today. Exodus 15 is one of the famous chapters in the Old Testament as it holds the most important, or one of the most vital songs ever sung in the history of Israel: The song of Moses. Right after they experienced the miraculous crossing through the red sea, Moses and the Israelites sang to God.

> "I will sing to the Lord, for he is highly exalted. Both horse and driver he has hurled into the sea. "The Lord is my strength and my defense; he has become my salvation. He is my God, and I will praise him, my father's God, and I will exalt him."
> Exodus 15:1-2 NIV

You'll notice that there's a sense of awe in their song that it seems like nobody can rob or take away anything. It is easy to praise God when you've just experienced a miracle, or everything is going well. That said, it is the case for the Israelites because just three days after this event they already grumbled against Moses and to the Lord.

> Then Moses led Israel from the Red Sea and they went into the Desert of Shur. For three days they traveled in the desert without finding water. When they came to Marah, they could not drink its water because it was bitter. (That is why the place is called Marah.) So the people grumbled against Moses, saying, "What are we to drink? Then Moses cried out to the Lord, and the Lord showed him a piece of wood. He threw it into the water, and the water became fit to drink. There the Lord issued a ruling and instruction for them and put them to the test. He said, "If you listen carefully to the Lord your God and do what is right in his eyes, if you pay attention to his commands and keep all his decrees, I will not bring on you any of the diseases I brought on the Egyptians, for I am the Lord, who heals you."
> Exodus 15:22-26 NIV

The Israelite's first response was to grumble the moment they experienced hardships and sufferings. A rather heartbreaking moment for me. Three things made it this way to me: (1)The Israelites experienced first-hand how great our God is, but still grumbled against Him. If there's a group of people who should know God's capabilities and strength, it should have been them. From how God sent plagues in Egypt and parted the red sea just to set them free from slavery, it wouldn't be that hard not to grumble. (2)This is an opportunity for them to believe that God is able. Hardships and trials are opportunities to worship God and believe in the impossible. It is also a chance to grow our faith as God molds us into the image of Jesus. (3) Lastly, it is heartbreaking because it is a picture of some of us today. Be it in wellness and comfort, they praise God, but our initial response was to grumble against God when trials followed. However, the good news is that God still delivered them from their hardships, and it will happen again and again.

God is our Jehovah-Rapha. He desires to heal us because He is our ultimate healer. In the same way with our doctors and physicians, we need to listen to their instructions and trust them. The best way to listen to God is through reading His written book. In the book of Matthew 4:4, "Jesus answered, "It is written: Man shall not live on bread alone, but on every word that comes from the mouth of God." You have to put the scripture of God into action, applied it to the problem, and pray God's word back to Him. You must believe the word is true and claim it is already done!

Because of this, God reminds the Israelites that He already spared them graciously and faithfully from the plagues on Egypt. In the same way, God wants us to continue listening and be obedient to His voice, and pay attention to Him—our ultimate redeemer and healer. God's healing power is not limited to your capacity to believe or capabilities to understand, rather God heals based on His divine will and purpose. He is now inviting you to wait and see that He can do wonders amidst your illness, pain, or anxiety. Our shortcomings, or lack of faith, will not hinder God from saving us. God is sovereign, and He is also merciful.

Four

SPEAK LIFE

*Gracious words are a honeycomb, sweet to the soul
and healing to the bones.
Proverbs 16:24 NIV*

Words matter, they can either create life or death. I remember my Granny telling me to be careful of what I say and think before I speak. The Scripture is clear, according to Proverbs 16:24, "Gracious Words are a honeycomb, sweet to the soul and healing to the bones." We have the assurance that our words have the power to heal. So, if you want a positive result, just remember to use optimistic statements and declare them. Pray for diving expectations that are not based on your experiences or situations.

One way to practice speaking life is by memorizing the Scriptures. The Bible says, "The spoken Word is life to the body" (John 6:63), and "Death and life are in the power of the tongue, and those that love it will eat of its fruit" (Proverbs 18:21). The Bible is a treasure trove filled with promises that we can use to speak positively and rightfully. The moment you memorize the verses or passages from the Bible, the Holy Spirit will prompt you and remind you of the promises God has for you. He will help you guard your lips as Proverbs 13:3 says, "Those who guard their lips preserve their lives, but those who speak rashly will come to ruin." Choose to speak life and allow the power of the Holy Spirit to work in your life.

Believing in faith, speaking positive and life-building aspirations into our lives is the authoritative power to heal, or it can be the power to destroy our destiny. Jesus tells us, "For by your words you will be justified, and by your words, you will be condemned" (Matthew 12:37). Our spoken words affect the mind, body, and spirit; it has the power to cast a blessing or curse. Confessing the Word of God in faith for your physical ailment, situation, or circumstance, name your request and claim that you are healed. Take it with expectation!

It is a written promise of God under the old and new covenant that our words have power, "My son, give attention to my words; Incline your ear to my sayings. Do not let them depart from your sight and keep them in your heart; they are life to those who find them and health to all their body. (Proverbs 4:20-22) Take hold to the word and boldly tell Him your needs, saying, Lord, you said in your word (locate a scripture that pertains to your need and stand in agreement); "For I will restore you to health and I will heal you of your wounds, declares the Lord," Jeremiah 30:17. God's words are true and He can't lie, yesterday, today, and forever.

So, boldly come to God with your petitions! Expect God to do what He says He will do according to His Word. We have not because we ask not. Call yourself healthy and say, "I declare and decree my body is healed through my faith and in accordance to God's Holy Word. Thank Him whether you see results or not. Healing is YOURS! He, Himself took out infirmities and carried away our diseases" (Matthew 8:17).

Five

Prayer for Healing & Deliverance

Beat your plowshares into swords and your pruning hooks into spears. Let the weakling say, "I am strong!"
Joel 3:10 NIV

Leonard Ravenhill said it perfectly, "Prayer is not a preparation for the battle; it is the battle." If I backed down or be dismayed the moment, I heard the nurses laughing at me, the surgery would have a different outcome.

Prayer is a battle. Our fight is not against flesh and blood, not against our sickness or diseases, but evil rulers and authorities in the unseen realm. The only way to battle it is through prayer and declaration. As Joel instructs the people of Israel, let's beat our plowshares, that is our voice and pruning hooks, our declaration.

So I invite you to pray and declare this prayer with me, and believe that it will be done by our Jehovah-Rapha, the God who heals.

PRAY AND DECLARE THIS PRAYER:

Father, In the name of Jesus Christ, I declare and decree that your healing power flows from (You) and I rebuke every sickness, disease, and unclean spirit that is attacking my body!

I refuse to allow any unclean spirit to take refuge in my body and the yoke is destroyed.

I stand in faith on your word believing I AM HEALED. Then select a healing scripture that you choose to claim for your healing **Lay hands on the body part that needs healing and command **name the sickness** to leave my body!

In the mighty name of Jesus, By His Stripes, I Am Healed. Amen

Six

30 Days of Healing Scriptures

*For I will restore health unto thee, and I will heal thee
of thy wounds, saith the LORD
Jeremiah 30:17 KJV*

This chapter will help you jumpstart a new habit and eventually become a healthy lifestyle of reading the Bible and praying through the Scriptures. Research has shown the power of prayer is powerful!

Take the next 30 days to meditate on God's promises, read each scripture, write your thoughts, and speak His promises over your situation until you receive your request. Expect that you will experience God every day for the rest of your life.

Day 01

*But He was wounded for our transgressions, He was bruised
for our iniquities; the chastisement for our peace
was upon Him, and by His stripes we are healed.
Isaiah 53:5*

Day 02

Is anyone among you sick? Let them call the elders of the church to pray over them and anoint them with oil in the name of the Lord. And the prayer offered in faith will make the sick person well; the Lord will raise them up. If they have sinned, they will be forgiven. Therefore confess your sins to each other and pray for each other so that you may be healed. The prayer of a righteous person is powerful and effective.
James 5:14-16

Day 03

O Lord, you alone can heal me; you alone can save.
My praises are for you alone!
Jeremiah 17:14

Day 04

You can find strength in God and His Word
"Let the weak say, 'I am strong.'"
Joel 3:10

Day 05

*My son, forget not my law; but let thine heart keep my commandments:
For length of days, and long life, and peace, shall they add to thee.*
Proverbs 3:1-2

_____
_____
_____
_____
_____
_____
_____
_____
_____
_____
_____
_____
_____
_____
_____
_____

Day 06

*Who Himself bore our sins in His own body on the cross,
that we, having died to sins, might live for
righteousness; by whose stripes you were healed.*
I Peter 2:24

Day 07

*The thief does not come except to steal, and to kill,
and to destroy. I have come that they may have life,
and that they may have it more abundantly.*
John 10:10

Day 08

Then Jesus told them, "I tell you the truth, if you have faith and don't doubt, you can do things like this and much more. You can even say to this mountain, 'May you be lifted up and thrown into the sea,' and it will happen. You can pray for anything, and if you have faith, you will receive it."
Matthew 21:21-22

_____
_____
_____
_____
_____
_____
_____
_____
_____
_____
_____
_____
_____
_____
_____
_____
_____

Day 09

And the Lord will take away from you all sickness.
Deuteronomy 7:15

Day 10

I shall live and not die, but live, and declare the works of the Lord.
Psalms 118:17

Day 11

The mouth of a righteous man is a well of life.
Proverbs 10:11

Day 12

My child, listen to me and do as I say,
and you will have a long, good life.
Proverbs 4:10

Day 13

So we fix our eyes not on what is seen, but on what is unseen, since what is seen is temporary, but what is unseen is eternal.
2 Corinthians 4: 18

Day 14

Christ redeemed us from the curse of the law by becoming a curse for us, for it is written: "Cursed is everyone who is hung on a pole." He redeemed us in order that the blessing given to Abraham might come to the Gentiles through Christ Jesus, so that by faith we might receive the promise of the Spirit... If you belong to Christ, then you are Abraham's seed, and heirs according to the promise.
Galatians 3:13-14, 29

Day 15

If you fully obey the Lord your God and carefully keep all his commands that I am giving you today, the Lord your God will set you high above all the nations of the world. 2 You will experience all these blessings if you obey the Lord your God
Deuteronomy 28: 1-2

Day 16

Do not fear, for I am with you; Do not anxiously look about you, for I am your God. I will strengthen you, surely I will help you, Surely I will uphold you with My righteous right hand.'... "For I am the Lord your God, who upholds your right hand, Who says to you, Do not fear, I will help you.
Isaiah 41:10,13

Day 17

What do you devise and [how mad is your attempt to] plot against the Lord? He will make a full end [of Nineveh]; affliction [which My people shall suffer from Assyria] shall not rise up the second time.
Nahum 1:9

Day 18

And behold, a leper came and worshiped Him, saying, "Lord, if You are willing, You can make me clean." Then Jesus put out His hand and touched him, saying, "I am willing; be cleansed." Immediately his leprosy was cleansed.
Matthew 8: 2-3

Day 19

Behold, I give you the authority to trample on serpents and scorpions, and over all the power of the enemy, and nothing shall by any means hurt you.
Luke 10:19

GOD'S PROMISES FOR HEALING

Day 20

I call heaven and earth as witnesses today against you, that I have set before you life and death, blessing and cursing; therefore choose life, that both you and your descendants may live; 20 that you may love the Lord your God, that you may obey His voice, and that you may cling to Him, for He is your life and the length of your days; and that you may dwell in the land which the Lord swore to your fathers, to Abraham, Isaac, and Jacob, to give them."
Deuteronomy 30:19-20

Day 21

*Beloved, I pray that you may prosper in all things
and be in health, just as your soul prospers.
3 John 2*

GOD'S PROMISES FOR HEALING

Day 22

He gives power to the weak and strength to the powerless... But those who trust in the Lord will find new strength. They will soar high on wings like eagles. They will run and not grow weary. They will walk and not faint.
Isaiah 40:29,31

_____
_____
_____
_____
_____
_____
_____
_____
_____
_____
_____
_____
_____
_____
_____
_____
_____
_____

Day 23

And everyone who calls on the name of the Lord will be saved.
Acts 2: 21

Day 24

With long life will I satisfy him and show him My salvation.
Psalm 91:16

Day 25

This is the confidence we have in approaching God: that if we ask anything according to his will, he hears us. And if we know that he hears us—whatever we ask—we know that we have what we asked of him.
1 John 5:14-15

Day 26

Jesus said to him, if you can believe, all things are possible to him who believes.
Mark 9:23

Day 27

Be anxious for nothing, but in everything by prayer and supplication, with thanksgiving, let your requests be made known to God; and the peace of God, which surpasses all understanding, will guard your hearts and minds through Christ Jesus.
Philippians 4:6-7

Day 28

*Trust in the Lord with all your heart;
do not depend on your own understanding.
Seek his will in all you do, and he will show you
which path to take. Don't be impressed with your
own wisdom. Instead, fear the Lord and turn away
from evil. Then you will have healing for your body
and strength for your bones.*
Proverbs 3:5-8

Day 29

*He forgives all my sins and heals all my diseases.
He redeems me from death and crowns me with love
and tender mercies. He fills my life with good things.
My youth is renewed like the eagles!
Psalm 103:3-5*

Day 30

If you will diligently hearken to the voice of the Lord your God and will do what is right in His sight, and will listen to and obey His commandments and keep all His statutes, I will put none of the diseases upon you which I brought upon the Egyptians, for I am the Lord who heals you.
Exodus 15:26

Seven

THE LORD'S PRAYER

But when you pray, go into your room, close the door and pray to your Father, who is unseen. Then your Father, who sees what is done in secret, will reward you.
Matthew 6:6 NIV

With only a few of the colors seen on their body and found only in seven states, cardinal birds are one of the birds you rarely see. It is said that when you see one, it signifies a spiritual messenger that brings you peace and hope; or a deceased loved one that wanted to visit you. There was a time when my grandfather, Meachino, taught me how to say a prayer and blow a kiss if ever I see such a bird. Passing this onto you that when you get to see a cardinal bird, I hope that you'll be encouraged to keep on pushing towards your healing. After all, they symbolize devotion and courage.

Similar to that of the cardinal bird, it is through praying that helped me to gain the courage to go through with the operation and claim healing in advance. It is by the power of prayer that we are encouraged by the Holy Spirit to keep pushing forward and Godward. As observed through the early disciples of Jesus, they're the ones who realized that the most vital part of a Christian is prayer. In Luke chapter 11, one of the disciples approached Jesus saying, "Lord, teach us to pray," this particular disciple saw in the lifestyle of Jesus that it is the most important thing for Him. If you look closely, you'll observe that they never asked Jesus to teach them how to heal, cast out demons, or make a sermon; they asked Him how to pray.

A lifestyle of prayer is just the fruit of our faith, not the root of faith. Jesus embodied that faith through Matthew 14:23, "After He had sent the crowds away, He went up on the mountain by Himself to pray; and when it was evening, He was there alone." Found also in Mark 1:35, "In the early morning, while it was still dark, Jesus got up, left the house, and went away to a secluded place, and was praying there." Also in Luke 5:16, "But Jesus Himself would often slip away to the wilderness and pray." We can go on and on, citing many verses in the life of Jesus, and still see that He always goes to a secluded place to be in an attitude of prayer. So it dawned on that disciple—who asked Jesus to teach them to pray—that prayer is the integral and most important practice of a Christian.

Just like everything else, there's also a wrong way of praying. Thus, it is also important to know the prayer that honors God and prayers that don't honor God. In Matthew chapter 6, Jesus explains to his disciples what prayer is not; starting at verse 5 through verse 8:

"And when you pray, do not be like the hypocrites, for they love to pray standing in the synagogues and on the street corners to be seen by others. Truly I tell you, they have received their reward in full. But when you pray, go into your room, close the door and pray to your Father, who is unseen. Then your Father, who sees what is done in secret, will reward you. And when you pray, do not keep on babbling like pagans, for they think they will be heard because of their many words. Do not be like them, for your Father knows what you need before you ask him."

The most effective and useful way of communicating with God would be through prayer. Just like the relationships we build, communication plays a key role in connecting us with others. However, to pray like the hypocrites and pagans alike, Jesus doesn't want you to do the same. Doing it like them, who loves to be seen praying, doesn't necessarily mean they are being heard by their gods; they aren't communicating, but all of it's just for show. Prayer, when practiced well, strengthens our relationship with the Father; it aligns our hearts to God the Father.

To make all of these possible and for us not to go astray, Jesus introduced to us the right way to pray. He said in verse 6, "When you pray, go into your room, close the door and pray to your Father." With that comes the question, "Why is prayer important for our healing?" Because in prayer, heaven invades the earth, and that place could be your room or your closet. Looking at Luke chapter 3 verse 21, "While [Jesus] was praying, heaven was opened." We get to experience heaven and divine healing when we pray. So how do we pray?

Jesus taught them to pray this:

The Lord's Prayer
Matthew 6:9-13
Our Father which art in heaven, Hallowed be
thy name.
Thy kingdom come, Thy will be done in earth,
as it is in heaven.
Give us this day our daily bread. And forgive us our debts, as we forgive our debtors. And lead us not into temptation, but deliver us from evil: For thine is the kingdom, and the power, and the glory, forever.
Amen.

Abba, Father, thank you for this great reminder. I would love to devote my time to prayer; exposing you to all my unbelief and sins, praising you and worshiping you; in spirit and truth. Guide me as I pray, lead me and teach me. Also, help me claim the miracle that You have instored in my life. Thank you.
In Jesus Name, Amen!

Eight

PSALM 23

*I am the good shepherd. The good shepherd sacrifices
his life for the sheep.*
John 10:11 NLT

One of the most famous and vital psalms in the Bible is Psalm 23. Scholars would say that this particular psalm is a hymn of confidence in God's compassion and care. Here, we can see two images of God as a Shepherd in this hymn: (1) A shepherd who takes care of his sheep; and (2) a master who takes care of his people. Let's read Psalm 23:

> The Lord is my shepherd;
> I shall not want.
> He makes me to lie down in green pastures;
> He leads me beside the still waters.
> He restores my soul;
> He leads me in the paths of righteousness
> For His name's sake.
> Yea, though I walk through the valley of the shadow of death,
> I will fear no evil;
> For You are with me;

Your rod and Your staff, they comfort me.
You prepare a table before me in the presence of
my enemies;
You anoint my head with oil;
My cup runs over.
Surely goodness and mercy shall follow me
All the days of my life;
And I will dwell in the house of the Lord
Forever.

Before becoming a successful king, David, who wrote this psalm, used to tend to his father's sheep; thus, making him conscious of how it's like to be a shepherd. Through it, David, who experienced God as his Good Shepherd, felt contented by it. Jesus in John chapter 10 spoke about him being the Good Shepherd, "I am the good shepherd. The good shepherd sacrifices his life for the sheep. A hired hand will run when he sees a wolf coming. He will abandon the sheep because they don't belong to him and he isn't their shepherd. And so the wolf attacks them and scatters the flock. The hired hand runs away because he's working only for the money and doesn't care about the sheep. (John 10:11-13)." Jesus, the Good Shepherd who walks with us, restores us, protects us—and even gave His life for us. He, who is always true to His words, will always meet our needs and be faithful to His promises.

Walking through valleys of several cases of illness, I have a Good Shepherd who leads me in green pastures and still waters. He, who comforted my heart and my eyes, they're always near to God alone. Simply knowing that He is my Good Shepherd secures me from any harm, empowers me to speak life, pray in the most difficult situations, and declare healing in my life.

God's promise to be a Good Shepherd is also for you. If you don't have this kind of relationship with God, the next chapter will be able to lead you into having a deeper relationship with Him, as a Father, and as a Good Shepherd.

Nine

SALVATION PRAYER

*Therefore, if anyone is in Christ, the new creation has come:
The old has gone, the new is here!
2 Corinthians 5:17 NIV*

Salvation Prayer

If you do not know Jesus as your Savior and Lord, simply pray the following prayer in faith, and Jesus will be your Lord!

Heavenly Father, I come to You in the Name of Jesus. Your Word says, "Whosoever shall call on the name of the Lord shall be saved," and "if thou shalt confess with thy mouth the Lord Jesus, and believe in thine heart that God hath raised him from the dead, thou shalt be saved" (Acts 2:21; Romans 10:9). You said my salvation would be the result of Your Holy Spirit giving me new birth by coming to live in me (John 3:5-6, 15-16; Romans 8:9-11) and that if I would ask, You would fill me with Your Spirit and give me the ability to speak with other tongues (Luke 11:13; Acts 2:4).

SALVATION PRAYER

I confess that Jesus is Lord, and I believe in my heart the You raised Him from the dead. Thank You for coming into my heart, for giving me Your Holy Spirit as You have promised, and for being Lord over my life. Amen.

Ten

HEALING PRAYER

Heal me, O Lord, and I shall be healed;
Save me, and I shall be saved,
For You are my praise.
Jeremiah 17:14 NKJV

Healing Prayer [READ PRAYER ALOUD]

Heavenly Father, I come to you in the name of my Lord and Savior, Jesus Christ. I resist every spiritual attack, infirmity, sickness, and disease that attacks my body! I refuse to allow any unclean spirit to take refuge in my mind, body, and spirit. I command the spirit of sickness and disease to leave my mind, body, and spirit immediately!

Satan, will not lord over me. In the mighty name of Jesus Christ, I declare and decree every evil work is destroyed and it shall NOT return! Lord, you said, If I call your name, you would answer me. Lord, I trust and believe in faith that you hear my prayer request and cast out every negative thought, doubt, and fear that lingers in my mind throughout the day. I pray that you will encamp your Angels of protection around me. Lord, I will wait patiently and expectantly for your healing touch. Father, your Word says, If I abide in you, you would abide in me; I am standing on your promises, according to, 1 Corinthians 15:57; thanks be to God, who gives us the victory, and in faith, I pray and agree with the expectation that by His stripes I am healed, Isaiah 53:4-5. In the name of Jesus, I ask and pray, Amen.

Scripture Reference List

Proverbs 4:20-22
Habakkuk 2:4
Psalm 1:2
Luke 11:28
John 16:23
Mathew 6:6
James 3:10
Jeremiah 30:17
Luke 8:43-48
Proverbs 17:22
Exodus 23:25-26
Genesis 6:3
Hebrews 13:8
Exodus 15:26 NIV
Exodus 15:1-2 NIV
Exodus 15:22-26 NIV
Matthew 4:4
Mark 3:10-11 NKJV
James 2:14-26
Psalm 112:1, 7
Luke 8:25
Romans 10:17
Galatians 3:13
Proverbs 16:24 NIV
Proverbs 16:24
John 6:63
Proverbs 18:21
Proverbs 13:3
Matthew 12:37
Proverbs 4:20-22
Jeremiah 30:17

SCRIPTURE REFERENCE LIST

Matthew 8:17
Joel 3:10 NIV
Jeremiah 30:17
Isaiah 53:4-5
James 5:14-16 (NIV)
Jeremiah 17:14 (NLT)
Joel 3:10
Proverbs 3:1-2
I Peter 2:24
John 10:10 (NKJV)
Matthew 21:21:22 (NLT)
Deuteronomy 7:15 (NKJV)
Psalm 118:17 (NKJV)
Proverbs 10:11
Proverbs 4:10 (NLT)
2 Corinthians 4:18 (AMP)
Galatians 3:13-14, 29 (NASB)
Deuteronomy 28:1-2 (AMP)
Isaiah 41: 10, 13 (NASB)
Nahum 1:9(b) (AMP)
Matthew 8: 2-3 (NKJW)
Luke 10:19 (NKJV)
Deuteronomy 30: 19-20 (NKJV)
3 John 2 (NKJV)
Isaiah 40:29, 31 (NLT)
Acts 2:21 (NIV)
Psalm 91:16 (NIV)
I John 5: 14-15
Mark 9:23 (NLT)
Philippians 4: 6-7
Proverbs 3:5-8 (NLT)
Psalm 103:3 (NLT)
Exodus 23:25 (NIV)

Matthew 6:6 NIV
Matthew 14:23
Mark 1:35
Luke 5:16
Matthew 6:5-8
Luke 3:21
Matthew 6:9-13
John 10:11 NLT
Psalm 23:1-6
John 10:11-13
2 Corinthians 5:17 NIV
Acts 2:21
Romans 10:9
John 3:5-6
John 3:15-16
Romans 8:9-11
Luke 11:13
Acts 2:4
Jeremiah 17:14 NKJV
1 Corinthians 15:57
Isaiah 53:4-5

Notes

Notes

Notes

Notes

Notes

If you appreciated this book, please let others know.
Share your thoughts and praise reports with us!

books@mlclegacy.com

About the Author

Dorita C. McDaniel—Rita—observed many healing miracles working in the medical field. She left that work to pursue her higher calling; helping students not only succeed, but excel as an Academic Advisor. She's also a Success Coach and spiritual advisor embracing a love of spreading the word of Jesus Christ. With an impressive list of degrees earned, she's an intelligent, well-spoken Christian woman who follows her belief and faith in God. This led her to write about the healing miracles she personally experienced as well as those she personally witnessed. She enjoys mentoring students, writing and researching her family's genealogy, studying and utilizing naturopathic medicine, aromatherapy, feeding the many beautiful birds that visit her home, and spending time with her tight-knit, loving family. Find out more about Rita at www.DCMcDaniel.com

Rita and Granddad

www.ingramcontent.com/pod-product-compliance
Lightning Source LLC
Chambersburg PA
CBHW071509070526
44578CB00001B/487